SUCCESS WITH AGAPANTHUS

Steven & Colin Hickman

2QT Limited (Publishing)

First Edition published 2018 by

2QT Limited (Publishing)

Settle, North Yorkshire BD24 9RH United Kingdom

The authors' website: www.somethingforthegarden.co.uk

Typeset and cover design by Hilary Pitt

Photography by kind permission of

Ian Thwaites

Dr P. F. Cooke - peterfcooke@ntlworld.com

Edward Barnham - www.holepark.com

Neil Hepworth on behalf of the Royal Horticultural Society

Peter Franklin

Bram Keyworth

Other photographs by Steven & Colin Hickman

Illustrations by: Leah Bilson - facebook.com/artbyleah

Printed in Slovenia by Latitude Press Ltd

A CIP catalogue record for this book is available
from the British Library

ISBN - 978-1-912014-05-7

CONTENTS

FOREWORD

In recent years the popularity of Agapanthus has increased beyond recognition, and much of this is surely down to the hard-work and dedication of the Hickman family who have totally embraced this wonderful plant

Steve and Elaine's passion for Agapanthus shines through in the visual feasts they create at shows, whether a stunning display of plants in full flower or an educational display showing visitors how to propagate and care for their plants.

The Hoyland Plant Centre is now synonymous with Agapanthus and it's great that Colin has joined his mum and dad in the family business. Not only do they hold a Plant Heritage National Collection, they are continually hybridising and creating new and exciting cultivars. One of the things they look for in new plants is hardiness and being based in Yorkshire you can rest assured that if it's a Hoyland Agapanthus, it will be perfect for growing in the UK climate.

Agapanthus in their native habitat.

I've had the pleasure to work with both Steve and Colin at many shows where they regularly give talks and practical demonstrations. The way Steve divides established clumps of Agapanthus with a meat clever is legendary and guaranteed to make the audience gasp! They live and breathe Agapanthus and their enthusiasm is infectious!

If you already grow Agapanthus or are thinking about getting some, this book is just what you need. It's up to date and full of the latest cultivars, cultural information, facts and growing tips to help you get the very best from your plants.

Martin Fish
Garden writer, broadcaster and RHS judge.

DEDICATION AND ACKNOWLEDGMENTS

This book is dedicated to Elaine Ann Hickman, without whom none of this would have been possible.

§

We would like to offer a huge thank you to the many institutions and individuals who have helped and encouraged us on our long journey to becoming highly respected and widely recognised Agapanthus and *Amaryllidaceae* specialists. Without which this book certainly would not have been possible.

Special mention must be made to Elaine and Heather Hickman whose hard work plays a major role in keeping the nursery running smoothly. A big thank you to Stephanie Barrett for her continued support and proof reading skills.

To our friend, author, actor, and writer Geoffrey Howse for both his initial encouragement to put pen to paper, and ongoing proof reading.

We would also like to thank our friends and fellow plant enthusiasts Ian Thwaites and Peter Cooke for sacrificing their time and talents to take many of the wonderful photographs in this book.

We would like to thank gardening expert and long-time friend Martin Fish, who has been instrumental with his encouragement and advice. Not to mention the rather flattering foreword.

Leah Bilson has sacrificed many hours to produce the amazing illustrations found throughout this book, we offer our warmest thanks and hope you continue to use your artistic talents in further work.

We would also like to thank the team at 2QT publishing, especially Catherine and Hilary for their guidance, hard work and patience throughout the process, it has been a pleasure to work with you both.

Last but by no means least, we would like to thank the Royal Horticultural Society for their continued support and recognition we have received over many years.

INTRODUCTION

During the last decade or so, the genus of Agapanthus has undergone a transformation from a seldom-seen, exotic perennial to one of the most widely grown plants in Britain, if not the world.

We, along with countless others, caught the Agapanthus 'bug', falling instantly in love. We have subsequently dedicated the last twenty years to growing countless thousands of Agapanthus in an effort to fill the gardens of Britain with this stunning plant.

Within this book we have drawn upon our own knowledge and experience and that of other experts in the field to provide an informative, yet easy to understand, guide to Agapanthus growing. We aim to dispel the myths and half-truths that have arisen regarding Agapanthus growing, and to provide a simple step-by-step approach to the cultivation and propagation of Agapanthus that will be useful for novice and expert alike.

Descriptions of what we feel are the most attractive and easy-to-grow varieties are provided, along with ideas on how best to use them. With its ability to thrive both in the garden and in containers, we believe there is always a place for Agapanthus – no matter how large or small the garden, patio, or balcony.

Agapanthus 'Midnight Dream'
Illustration by Leah Bilson

WHAT IS AN AGAPANTHUS?

The word Agapanthus comes from the Greek AGAPE, 'love', and ANTHOS, 'flower', hence its common name, 'flower of love' – an apt name, we feel, for such a well-loved and widely grown plant.

Agapanthus have now spread far and wide across the globe. Yet they are truly native only to South Africa and nowhere else. They belong to the Amaryllidaceae, a large family mainly confined to Southern Africa.

There are six main species of Agapanthus recognised by science: A. PRAECOX, A. AFRICANUS, A. CAMPANULATUS, A. CAULESCENS, A. CODDII, and A. INAPERTUS. They have a very wide natural distribution in South Africa, extending all the way from the Cape Peninsula, which lies within the Western Cape province, to Limpopo at the north-eastern corner of the country. Some species are found within a limited geographical area, whilst others are widespread. Agapanthus are found in a range of habitats, from arid areas to more moist environments with year-round rainfall.

When we visit the volcanic slopes of Madeira or gaze upon the legions of Agapanthus praecox lining the hedgerows and sand dunes of Tresco on the Isles of Scilly, it is difficult to believe that they are not natives in those places, but alien invaders brought there by the discerning gardeners of bygone times. Forms of A. praecox are now extremely widespread throughout Mediterranean Europe, West Coast USA, Australia, and New Zealand; in some of these hot climates the species is sometimes even considered invasive! Horticulturalists often comment that Agapanthus seem to have spread with greater success in the wider world than they ever did within their South African homeland.

Naturalised Agapanthus, Lisbon, Portugal.

All Agapanthus are perennials – thus, given satisfactory growing conditions, should flourish for many years. Contrary to popular belief, Agapanthus do not grow from a 'bulb' that most gardeners would recognise but from a strange rhizome-like structure: a fleshy horizontal stem that grows on or just below soil level and is attached to a typically thick, fleshy, well-developed root system. There is nothing quite like dividing your very first Agapanthus, revealing the rhizome and root structure. I can only describe it as looking like a giant cigar that has been sat on for some time by a rather large individual. Agapanthus typically start from a single rhizome and in time form a large clump with many rhizomes growing together, often one on top of the other.

Agapanthus all exhibit the same characteristic green, strap-like foliage. However, unbeknown to many gardeners, they are divided into two distinct categories.

Elongated Rhizome-like structure of an Agapanthus.

Rhizomes growing in groups as the plant matures.

EVERGREEN TYPES, which are native to either winter or year-round rainfall areas, are typically, yet not always, characterised by large, broad fleshy leaves that persist all year round, usually held upon thick, fleshy stems.

DECIDUOUS TYPES abound in areas of summer or seasonal rainfall. As a result, these tend to die back completely during winter. They are often characterised by having much narrower, finer leaves than evergreen types. They exhibit a multitude of stems, but of a much smaller size than a typical evergreen Agapanthus.

There are also variegated-foliage varieties of both evergreen and deciduous types, which boast typically beautiful flowers, held atop attractive bright silver or gold variegated foliage.

The flowers of Agapanthus are just as variable, ranging in height from a lowly 6 inches (15cm) to over 7 feet (213cm), with flower heads varying in size between 3 inches (7.5cm) and 1.2 feet (35cm), depending on variety. The flower heads, or umbels, are made up of a multitude of individual flowers, which appear to separate as the flower emerges from the characteristic bud, or calyx. Flower form also varies greatly. Some flower heads are a tight clustered globe, some a more open, loose sphere, and others are nodding or fully pendulous.

By far the most striking difference between varieties is that of flower colour. Many of us in the days of old were first introduced to, and became familiar with, the traditional large mid-blue Agapanthus, then, perhaps, after a suitable period had passed, acquired a white form if we were feeling particularly adventurous. Today it is a different story altogether; the sheer range and depth of colours is truly mind-boggling. They are available in colours ranging from pure white with flushes of pink to steely grey, pale sky blue, mauve, navy blue, indigo, and deep purples that border on black. There are even bi-colour varieties available with shades of blue and white in the same flower.

Typical form of many evergreen Agapanthus.

Typical form of many deciduous Agapanthus.

Bright foliage of a variegated Agapanthus.

The myriad, sizes, forms, and colours of Agapanthus.

Steven Hickman with a giant Agapanthus praecox near Penzance, Cornwall.

Though vastly different in appearance, all Agapanthus require very similar growing conditions and are not a demanding plant to grow. We believe a gardener of any experience level can successfully grow any of these stunning varieties. We have learned through hard work and experience to follow a few key principles, and get the basics right.

Agapanthus 'Chelsea Blue'
Illustration by Leah Bilson

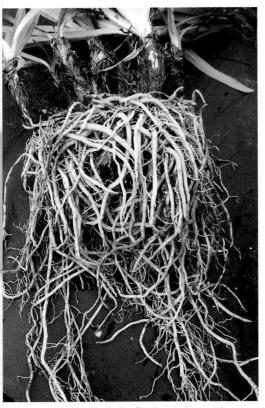

The thick, fleshy root system, utilised by indigenous peoples.

We would not recommend you use Agapanthus for medicinal purposes as they are currently not approved by modern medicine. The indigenous peoples of South Africa made no clear distinction between medicinal, spiritual, and symbolic uses for Agapanthus and there remains a strong belief in its many benefits, especially regarding fertility and childbirth.

It is curious to think that a plant we in the Western world prize purely for its beauty and ornamental appeal is valued principally for its practical uses in its place of origin.

In cultivation

THE VERY FIRST Europeans to gaze upon Agapanthus were men of the Dutch East India Company who set up a trading station at the Cape of Good Hope in 1652. The first plants taken back to Europe were likely that of the evergreen Agapanthus africanus.

It wasn't until the mid-1700s, when explorers such as the Swedes Carl Peter Thunberg and Anders Sparrman and English plant hunter Francis Masson, himself a disciple of the famous director of the Royal Botanic Gardens at Kew, Sir Joseph Banks, braved the alien climate and hostile local wildlife to travel further east across South Africa, that other species of Agapanthus were discovered and brought into cultivation.

Agapanthus were first cultivated in the Netherlands as early as the 1680s in the Hortus Medicus Garden in Amsterdam and Leiden Botanical Garden.

It is thought that Agapanthus were first introduced to Britain from Holland by Princess Mary of England, who had married the Dutch King Willem III.

Agapanthus steadily became more widely grown during the nineteenth century as the British Empire expanded into new territories. Botanical Garden planners and wealthy Victorians alike had an insatiable appetite for new and exotic-looking perennials, and would plant them extensively within gardens and glasshouses.

A much wider range of Agapanthus became available during the mid twentieth century. The plantsman Lewis Palmer was able to acquire a large amount of seed, which he obtained from a collection of wild Agapanthus on a trip to Kirstenbosch Botanical Garden in South Africa. From these Palmer went on to breed and propagate many beautiful

Early illustration of
Agapanthus africanus
Botanical Magazine vol. 14 (1800)

Above: Agapanthus 'Midnight Star' at Raveningham Hall, Norfolk

Below: Mixed Agapanthus borders at Raveningham Hall, Norfolk

varieties, some of which were hardier and able to survive outdoors during winter. An increased interest in Agapanthus is attributed to the Royal Horticultural Society Wisley plant trial held during the 1970s, which contained many of Palmer's varieties. New and exciting hardy varieties were also bred elsewhere in England. For example, at Raveningham Hall in Norfolk Lady Priscilla Bacon produced the well-known Star series, containing varieties such as 'Arctic Star' and 'Midnight Star', which continue to be widely planted and admired to this day.

This trend in Agapanthus breeding continued in the later part of the twentieth and into the twenty-first century, helped by the creation in 1978 of NCCPG (National Council for the Conservation of Plants and Gardens). Now known by the much simpler title of Plant Heritage, this organisation focused on the development of the National Plant Collection scheme, which enabled nurseries and institutions to focus on breeding and acquiring larger plant collections. Its aim was to conserve the plant species and hybrids for future generations as a sort of living library.

From the early twenty-first century, through increased media exposure, the growth of plant retail markets and the expansion of flower shows have undoubtedly played a significant role in increasing the popularity of Agapanthus, enabling gardeners to appreciate them in all their splendour.

The story of Hoyland Plant Centre

HOYLAND PLANT CENTRE is currently run by husband and wife Steven and Elaine Hickman and their son Colin. The story began when newlyweds Steven and Elaine acquired a boggy field adjacent to their home near Barnsley in South Yorkshire during the early 1980s. The subsequent years were spent improving the site and adding glasshouses and polytunnels in order to grow a range of trees, shrubs, and perennials to supply our landscaping business. As the nursery grew in size, we also began to provide a range of wholesale plants to many other garden centres and nurseries throughout the UK.

Around twenty years ago we began selling our plants at various flower shows and plant fairs. It was at one of these plant fairs that Steve and Elaine's youngest daughter, Heather, bought a striking-looking perennial as a birthday present for her father. Steve and Elaine both fell in love with this breathtaking specimen, which happened to have one blue flower stem and one white within the same container. This plant was our very first Agapanthus praecox and was the start of our ongoing fascination with Agapanthus.

Before long we had ceased to grow such a broad range of nursery stock, instead focusing all our efforts on becoming a specialist nursery growing only Agapanthus and a select group of related species, the majority being native to South Africa. During this time our collections of both Agapanthus and the related genus of Tulbaghia were awarded National Collection status by Plant Heritage.

Nursery stock
on the point of
flowering

Above: Agapanthus stock beds
in all their splendour.

Left: The hardy Agapanthus
National Collection at the
nursery.

Exhibiting Agapanthus

AROUND TEN YEARS ago we began the daunting challenge of exhibiting Agapanthus at the prestigious RHS Flower Shows. A highlight of this journey came in 2016 when our educational exhibit of Agapanthus and Nerine was awarded a Gold medal at the Chelsea Flower Show – no mean feat considering both Agapanthus and Nerine are late-summer-flowering perennials and Chelsea Flower Show is held in spring. As such, a combination of heating, grow lights, and the selection of early-flowering cultivars was necessary to flower Agapanthus and Nerines out of their natural season.

An exceptional year for us was 2017. We achieved Gold medals at every RHS Flower Show, with our Linley Exhibit at Chelsea Flower

Below: Our RHS Master Grower exhibit at Chatsworth Flower Show 2017 featuring not only Agapanthus but a whole host of other plants we grow at the Nursery, these include Tulbaghia, Nerine, Amarine, Clivia, Dierama and a myriad of South African bulbs and succulent plants.

Show achieving the award of Best Educational Exhibit of 2017. We also became one of only a handful of nurseries ever to receive the prestigious RHS Master Grower Award. Consequently, we were invited to stage a large and elaborate exhibit at the first ever RHS Chatsworth Flower Show. This coincided with a piece of major coverage on BBC Gardeners' World. This was daunting in the extreme, yet proved to be invaluable and immensely rewarding.

Our aim is not only to provide high-quality plants but also to educate gardeners. We try to use our exhibits to inspire people to use Agapanthus in unique and exciting ways. This has been a huge privilege and a remarkable journey for us. We hope the future will be just as thrilling and rewarding.

Left: Our educational exhibit of Nerine and Amarine at Chatsworth Flower Show 2017.

Below: Our floral exhibit, Tatton Park Flower Show 2017.

Our 2017 Gold Medal winning Agapanthus educational exhibit at
Chelsea Flower Show 2017

Agapanthus 'Margaret'
Illustration by Leah Bilson

GROWING AGAPANTHUS

Soils and growing media

Perhaps the most important requirement for successful Agapanthus cultivation is providing the correct soil type. A well-drained sand or silt loam is ideal, though most garden soils are adequate.

People often lose Agapanthus during winter, which has given rise to the belief that they are frost tender. Actually they are very resistant to frost, but are susceptible to winter wet. You should not plant Agapanthus directly into a heavy clay soil, which is prone to waterlogging during winter and drought during summer. A slow and prolonged demise is often seen if you plant an Agapanthus in heavy clay soil – the plant will not usually die after a single year, but will get gradually weaken over two or three years before finally giving out entirely. A sad outcome for all involved.

All is not lost, however, if you suspect you have heavy clay yet are determined to grow Agapanthus in the garden; there are options available. The soil can be improved by the incorporation of a plentiful supply of organic matter in the form of well-rotted manure, compost, leaf mould, or fresh topsoil. It is also advisable to mix in grit, horticultural sand, or perlite to 'open up' the soil structure, which will improve drainage in winter and aid water retention in the summer. Raised beds are also commonly used atop heavy clay soil to give new plants the opportunity to establish in a well-drained growing media. If all this sounds like rather hard work (it does to us) then simply dig a hole, plunge a pot-grown Agapanthus into that hole (pot and all) and leave in situ for the growing season. Having done

this, simply lift it from the border at the end of October before the wet and cold weather arrives.

An increasingly popular option is to grow Agapanthus in containers, where they will thrive if treated correctly. Unfortunately, this is where the confusion often starts. Some growers say to pot on regularly; others say they require restriction and will only truly thrive when incredibly pot bound. It is true that overly pot-bound plants often exhibit a marked reduction in both plant vigour and the number of flowers each year. This is often due to inadequate space and nutrients in the remaining soil. At the other extreme, however, overpotted plants will often take a very

Top: Heavy clay soil
Left: The perfect sandy loam soil

Above: If you have heavy clay soil, a trick is to plunge the pot in the ground, lifting in the autumn before the weather turns wet and cold.

Below: Overly pot-bound plant in dire need of division.

Above left: A well-developed 9cm plant ideal for potting on.
Above right: A trio of plants is ideal for a 10 litre pot.

Below: A single plant is ideal in a 3 litre pot.

long time to establish and flower, as they struggle to fill a pot that is far too large.

The answer seems to lie somewhere in between the two extremes. Over the years we have found that young plants or small divisions of perhaps one to two years old do indeed benefit from root restriction within a small pot of perhaps 9–11cm in diameter. However, once an established root system has developed to fill the pot, then further root restriction is no longer necessary and can even hinder growth and flowering.

When the root system has developed sufficiently, it is worth potting on the young plant into a larger pot. From a 9–11cm pot to a 3 litre pot is advisable. A popular option is to plant a trio of 9cm size plants into a large 10–12 litre pot. They will grow together and give a much more impressive display far sooner than would a lone specimen.

As a rule of thumb, we recommend potting on your Agapanthus every two years and dividing them every four years. When potting on, the ideal mix for Agapanthus is a 2:1 ratio of two parts multipurpose

The perfect potting mix of 2 parts compost to 1 part grit.

compost or John Innes No. 2 or 3 to one part horticultural grit or perlite. This creates a fertile, open, free-draining growing medium in which Agapanthus really thrive. Good drainage is crucial. So always ensure the container has adequate drainage holes. A shallow layer of crocks or coarse grit can also be added to the bottom of the container to further enhance drainage.

Aspect

MANY OF US conjure up an image in our minds of Agapanthus basking in the sunshine of a south-facing border or sunny patio. Whilst they undoubtedly enjoy the sunnier parts of the garden as many South African plants do, there is still some degree of flexibility regarding where to place Agapanthus within the garden.

Providing the soil conditions are favourable, Agapanthus will often flourish in south-, south-west-, south-east-, and north-west-facing borders, or containers, so long as they receive direct sunlight for some portion of the day. Agapanthus can even grow in somewhat deeper shade, such as directly beneath a canopy of trees, though a consequence of this is the tendency of both the foliage and flowers to bend as they lean towards the light. A reduction in the number and

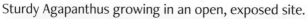

Sturdy Agapanthus growing in an open, exposed site.

Agapanthus growing in shade will lean towards the sun.

quality of flowers can also occur if the shade is extremely dense with no direct sunlight.

Agapanthus do look somewhat top-heavy and fragile when in full flower, but modern varieties are structurally very strong and are able to withstand strong winds without the need for staking or support. If treated correctly, they can thrive even in the most exposed sites.

Winter care

THE TRADITIONAL, YET misleading, view that Agapanthus are frost tender has now been proven false. This is thanks to factors such as increased knowledge of Agapanthus cultivation requirements, milder winters, and a greater range of varieties. This means that Agapanthus can now be successfully overwintered outdoors, with a little bit of know-how.

Most evergreen Agapanthus, providing they are planted in a reasonably free-draining soil, are frost hardy to at least -5°C.

Top: Deciduous Agapanthus should die back in November.
Above: Cut back to 2 inches in November.
Below: A mulch of chipped bark will protect the plant from severe frosts.

Deciduous types, which die back completely in winter, are far tougher and can withstand temperatures to at least -10°C. That said, a useful general rule for British gardeners is to draw an artificial line across Britain between The Wash in East Anglia on the East Coast to the Severn Estuary in the South West. If you are beneath this imaginary line (the southern half of the country), you will most likely be able to grow both evergreen and deciduous types in either the garden, containers, or both with little winter protection. If you are above the line (the northern half), it is best to think of deciduous types as a hardy border perennial and evergreens as somewhat tender. These are best grown in pots where they can be readily protected in the coldest of winters.

This is of course only a general rule. If you have a mild microclimate, live in a coastal area, or live in a city then you will be likely to have lighter frosts than someone in an exposed upland area or a frost pocket, regardless of where you are in the country.

In areas where prolonged and heavy frosts are prevalent, additional protection can be afforded to Agapanthus. If deciduous types are planted in the ground then it is advisable to cut the foliage back to about 3cm above ground level, and cover with a mulch. A simple layer of chipped bark, straw, or compost is ideal. The harder the frosts, the deeper the mulch layer is a good principle to follow; anything from 5cm to 20cm can be applied at the beginning of November, then gently brushed aside in late March as the new growth points begin to emerge.

Evergreen types should be brought inside a cold glasshouse or unheated room. People often make the mistake of bringing them into the house during winter as a precaution against the frost. This might seem a good idea, but a house is usually far too warm for Agapanthus as a cool winter is required to initiate flowering. Many gardeners now simply wrap the plant, container and all, in fleece or hessian, then place it next to the house or in the lee of a sheltered wall, which usually provides sufficient winter protection.

Evergreen Agapanthus can be wrapped in fleece then moved to a sheltered spot.

When overwintering Agapanthus, we have found it is often worth planning for the worst whilst hoping for the best. All over Britain hard frosts have become much less frequent and severe, which is often put down to global warming. In recent years we have left evergreen Agapanthus outside in Yorkshire all year round with no adverse effects whatsoever. Throughout the country people are doing the same by giving their Agapanthus little or no winter protection. Even so, we recommend that gardeners be willing and able to protect their plants should a harsh winter beckon.

Watering

Agapanthus are drought tolerant and somewhat forgiving of
neglect, especially compared to many other herbaceous perennials.
None the less, they still benefit from ample water during the growing
season (March to October) if they are to thrive.

Well-established specimens require less supplementary watering than
young plants that are newly planted. We find that regular watering
is usually only necessary in the height of summer, when hot weather
and drought are likely for periods. This of course can depend on
the soil conditions found within the garden. A rich loam soil, with
plenty of organic matter, will certainly hold on to moisture much
better than a soil that is predominantly sand or clay. Furthermore,
it is worth considering your location within Britain and the amount
of rainfall you usually receive annually. For example, a garden in
South East England, one of the driest parts of Britain, will likely
have a heavy clay soil, which is prone to rapid drying. As a result,
it will need far more supplementary watering than, say, a garden in
the North West of England or Ireland, where the soil is often richer
and more water retentive whilst also receiving more than twice the
annual rainfall of South East England. Agapanthus require very little
watering during winter as they are dormant. If they are planted in
the ground, they can be ignored until spring; if in containers, all
Agapanthus should be soaked thoroughly in mid-November then kept
slightly moist throughout the winter.

Feeding

One aspect of Agapanthus growing that breeds confusion is whether
they should be fed or not. Like the majority of garden plants,
Agapanthus do indeed benefit from feeding, but they have very
specific requirements.

A common mistake made by gardeners is to be too kind to Agapanthus. Many committed gardeners diligently feed their plants once every two weeks, usually with balanced general-use plant feed, then eagerly await their well-deserved blooms. These often fail to appear, much to the gardener's dismay. Balanced feeds are undoubtedly of great benefit to a broad range of garden plants, but they contain far too much nitrogen for Agapanthus. The result is copious amounts of lush green foliage, but with few or no flowers.

We have found that Agapanthus require large quantities of potash (potassium) to flower consistently year on year. Various methods of application can be used to achieve this, such as slow-release granular feeds applied in spring, and more regular use of liquid feeds. A common practice is the regular application of tomato feed. Whilst this is a better option than using a balanced feed, tomato feed does not seem to have sufficient potash levels to fully satisfy Agapanthus, which are incredibly hungry for potash.

Top: Water soluble high potash (K) feed.

Bottom: Thoroughly drench roots and leaves.

For this reason, we have produced our own specialist Agapanthus feed, which contains up to four times the quantity of potash than most tomato feeds whilst also containing many other nutrients and understanding. It is essential to follow simple practices such as the prompt removal of infected plant material, which should be burned or disposed of appropriately. Propagation tools should also be cleaned and sterilised after each use to avoid spreading disease and virus as the plants are split and moved.

Pest and diseases

FORTUNATELY for the gardener, Agapanthus is one of those plants that are relatively untroubled by the ever-increasing host of pests and diseases that affect our gardens. As is often the case, a healthy, well-nurtured plant will often grow trouble-free, only succumbing to a pest and disease problem if the overall health and vigour of the plant deteriorates, through factors such as severe drought or poor soil.

Plants in poor health can be affected by insects, for example, APHIDS, MEALY BUGS, GREEN FLY, AND SCALE INSECTS. If given the correct conditions, a plant will often recover from insect infestations with little treatment. More severe infestations can either be treated with an insecticide or cleaned off manually using soapy water. There is a new insect known as the agapanthus GALL MIDGE, which can cause the dieback of individual flowers or whole flower heads. Though little is known about this pest, it is not thought to be widespread within British gardens. If found, infected flowers should be removed and burned.

Fungal diseases such as Phytophthora and Botrytis can affect Agapanthus if they are exposed to wet, humid conditions for prolonged periods. If a fungal infection is caught early, repeated doses of fungicide is usually effective.

Viruses can also infect Agapanthus, though the detrimental effects of these are negligible. Newer varieties bought from a reputable supplier are usually virus free.

Good garden hygiene is a very important yet often overlooked

Agapanthus 'Artic Star'
Illustration by Leah Bilson

AGAPANTHUS PROPAGATION

Agapanthus propagation is immensely rewarding and yet simple to undertake. It can reinvigorate old, tired clumps, and give you many more plants to use in the garden. It will undoubtedly make you very popular among friends and family when you bestow upon them your surplus plants. For us at Hoyland Plant Centre, propagation is one of the most interesting and fulfilling jobs of the many we undertake here at the nursery. Whether we are dividing a mature clump of an unusual variety, or sowing specially selected seeds to obtain new and interesting hybrids, there is no doubt that there is something special about gaining many Agapanthus from a few initial plants or a single packet of seeds.

Division

AGAPANTHUS, ALONG WITH a vast range of other perennials, can be readily divided. Agapanthus do not come true from seed so division is the best method of propagation, especially for a named variety, which is often grown for a specific feature, such as height, form, or colour.

Division is not only an easy way to multiply your number of Agapanthus but it is also a necessary task to undertake in order to keep mature plants vigorous and flowering well, as is the case with many other perennials. Overly mature specimens see a gradual reduction in the size and abundance of flowers, with the central inhabitants of the clump declining as they are congested by the young vigorous growth that surrounds them. Dividing your Agapanthus will also make them more manageable. You will understand what I mean if you have ever tried to prise from a pot, or lift from the border, a huge ten-year-old specimen that should have been divided years ago. Such a task damages the morale and back in equal measure – while all too often resulting in the costly loss of a rather large and expensive terracotta pot!

It is true that Agapanthus can be successfully divided at any time throughout the growing season. Through experience we have found that the best time to do so is spring. Between mid-March and mid-May is ideal. This is for two reasons: first, we believe that dividing in spring gives them the best chance of successful establishment, as they have the rest of the growing season in which to recover; second, by spring the flower bud is well developed within the plant and will flower that same summer and continue to flower in subsequent years, regardless of division. By contrast, Agapanthus that are divided later in summer or after flowering often will not flower the following year, only producing foliage as they re-establish and settle in. Agapanthus can be divided down to individual growth points or 'eyes' if your aim is to obtain as many small specimens as possible. However, it is often best to only divide a large Agapanthus into say four to six pieces. That way they stand the greatest chance of survival and will be much quicker to re-establish and flower.

1. Remove the plant from the container or lift from the soil.
2. Work out in advance the points where the cuts will be made.
3. Use a clean and sharp tool (spade, cleaver, knife, or saw) to make a clean cut with minimal wounding. Always ensure that at least one growth point is present on the rhizome segment.
4. Ideally, leave the fresh division at least 24 hours to 'rest'. This allows the wound to dry out, reducing the chance of disease.

5. Pot up or replant the divisions into a fresh, well-drained growing medium.
6. Water in thoroughly to ensure good root-to-soil contact.

Colin Hickman potting up fresh divisions.

Growing from seed

RAISING AGAPANTHUS FROM seed is an excellent way to obtain large numbers of new plants, though it will take much longer to reach a flowering size plant compared to division, as seedlings often take up to four years to reach maturity and flowering size. You can see why growing Agapanthus from seed is considered the pursuit of the patient gardener! It is also true that Agapanthus do not come true from seed. Put simply, a mother plant may be pollinated by any other Agapanthus in the area. The resultant offspring will not be identical to either parent plant. Some proportion of the offspring will closely resemble the parent plant, yet equally many may exhibit very different characteristics in flower colour, height, form, growth habit, and hardiness. That said, some of the best and most well-loved varieties have come from either deliberate or incidental hybrid crosses. We encourage gardeners to try their hand at raising their own Agapanthus from seed; they may very well end up with many new and unique plants, which will undoubtedly serve to enhance and beautify the garden.

Even if you do not have the time or inclination to sow your Agapanthus seed, all is not lost. Agapanthus will self-seed in the garden. This means that ripe seed heads will simply drop their seeds in the garden as they are buffeted and battered by the winter weather. Opting to leave the old seed heads on the plant until spring will not affect the plant's future growth or flowering. As the soil warms, fallen seeds will germinate in situ, with some growing to maturity if the conditions are suitable. Far fewer seedlings are obtained from self-seeding than from seed sowing under glass, but zero effort is required. If you want to sow Agapanthus seed, it is best done within a year of harvesting, while the seeds are still fresh and viable.

1. When the seed pods have turned a russet brown, and cracked open to reveal the small black seeds, they are ready for harvesting. Place a bag over the top of the seed head and cut from the plant. The seed can then be shaken into the bag, which will contain the seeds.

2. Prepare a suitable growing media, such as John Innes seed sowing compost or sieved multi-purpose compost.

3. Fill the seed tray with the potting mix. Small numbers of seeds can be sown in a plant pot.

4. The germination rate for Agapanthus is high, so they should be sown thinly over the soil surface; then covered with a fine layer of compost (just enough to cover the seed).

5. The seed tray can then be watered in, placed in a greenhouse or sunny windowsill, and kept moist.

6. Agapanthus seeds can take up from 4 to 6 weeks to germinate. The seedlings can be pricked out into 9cm pots after around 6 months.

Micropropagation

Micropropagation is a method commonly used by growers to obtain large numbers of generally identical plants. Under laboratory conditions, tiny fragments of the mother plant are taken and placed in a sterile growing medium. In time, these tissues grow into a small plant, which is identical to the mother plant. The easiest/best way to produce an exact clone of a specific plant is the best. Whilst division is still used by us and by many other growers, it can be time consuming and relies upon large numbers of stock plants, which can be slow to clump up. Thus, micropropagation has given us a means by which to propagate very quickly large quantities of the best varieties, which would otherwise only be available in small numbers and at a premium price.

Furthermore, micropropagation has the added benefit of producing clean, virus-free plant material, which is not always the case with division.

Young plantlets ideal for growing on.

Agapanthus 'Moonlight Star'
Illustration by Leah Bilson

HOW TO USE
AGAPANTHUS

A gapanthus are one of the most versatile of garden plants, lending themselves to the garden, containers, and even cut flower arrangements with equal effectiveness.

A garden is a very personal space. A place where you can stamp your mark. Our different personalities are reflected in how we like to garden and what plants we find attractive. Far be it from us to tell you what Agapanthus you should plant and how you should garden with them. But for those who would like ideas and inspiration, we hope this chapter is of some use to you.

Agapanthus in containers

AGAPANTHUS MAKE EXCELLENT container plants, and it is well worth positioning them in a conspicuous location so they can receive the attention they deserve. Whether it be a formal courtyard, terrace, or small or urban garden or balcony, there is truly an Agapanthus to suit all needs.

The brilliant colour and architectural nature of Agapanthus mean they can be used individually, with a single specimen in a lone container, or as a grouping of numerous plants, often incorporating different varieties within the same container. Larger-growing praecox types are often better in their own container. The great advantage of containers is that they are easily moved. Therefore, it is wise to place your containerised Agapanthus close together. The colours, sizes, and forms will complement one another beautifully to make the most dramatic effects. Using different varieties to create both interest and contrast is very effective. Yet, so is the use of a single variety in repetition – it can add an air of formality to an area, providing a continuity of colour and form that some of us seek. If space is very limited, dwarf varieties look wonderful planted in window boxes and, unlike commonly used bedding plants, will persist for many years.

Both here at the nursery and on our many exhibits, we have experimented with a huge variety of containers, some of which are commonplace whilst others have been new and somewhat experimental. There is an extensive range of containers available to the gardener, and often the choice depends on what sort of a style or mood is being sought.

For a more formal look the most commonly used containers are clay (terracotta) or glazed pots. If the area in question is of a very limited size then a single pair of these pots flanking a door, lawn, or gate can add a sense of formality with very little effort. If the space is more generous then they can be placed together in groups or in rows flanking a lawn, path, or border. Urns are also very dramatic when attempting to create a formal look, and have the added benefit of providing extra height to a specimen, especially if the urn is raised on a plinth.

For a softer, more informal look, a vast range of containers is readily available. Plastic and imitation clay pots are both cheap and effective. For more long-term planting, oak half barrels make generous containers and certainly have rustic appeal. We have had great success using reclaimed containers such as dolly tubs, watering cans, milk jugs, wheelbarrows, and even a small sailboat. If you are creative enough, the choice is truly endless.

An old, tired rowboat makes a generous planter.

Above: Smaller Agapanthus
varieties are ideal for troughs and
window boxes.

Left: Large terracotta pots can
create a formal look.

Below: Blue glazed planters
complement Agapanthus blooms
perfectly.

Recycled metal planters achieve a contemporary look.

Agapanthus in the garden

AGAPANTHUS MAKE OUTSTANDING garden perennials in most parts
of Britain, though in colder areas deciduous varieties are certainly
much easier to grow in the garden as they are significantly more frost
hardy. Even the inclusion of a single plant can enhance any planting
scheme, such is the boldness and beauty of Agapanthus. Better yet is
the mass planting of a single variety, which creates a very dramatic
effect – though a large area is often needed to fully achieve this.
Mass planting in such a way is particularly useful when attempting
to develop a strong colour scheme within a garden; a mass of white,
blue, or purple flowers makes quite a statement in any garden.
Especially when the flower heads are covered in bees and other
pollinators on a warm summer's day.

A popular option is to plant a mix of different varieties together,
where differences both subtle and striking can be appreciated. This
also allows the gardener to make good use of a plant's individual

Hardy British varieties planted en masse.

characteristics, such as height, form, and colour. The simple use of taller varieties towards the back of a border and more compact ones closer to the front adds a tiered effect and allows all varieties to be viewed without the smaller ones being blocked out by their taller neighbours. This also creates a layering effect, which gives the whole scheme a softer, more naturalistic look.

Equally beautiful yet infinitely more useful are the variegated Agapanthus varieties. These can either be planted as individual specimens or incorporated into a wider planting scheme. They are very effective when planted alongside green-leaved varieties, where the striking silver and gold foliage breaks up and softens an otherwise dense area of deep green foliage.

A variety known as Agapanthus patens is extremely useful as it seems to grow in deeper shade than other Agapanthus, with no adverse effects.

Above: A riot of different
varieties complement and
contrast with one another.

Right: Hight impact mass
planting of a single variety.

Planting combinations

WHILST ANY INDIVIDUAL or group of Agapanthus is undoubtedly attractive, there are certain combinations of varieties that are proven winners, creating an effect that truly enhances the overall appeal of each variety used. It is just as important to combine Agapanthus varieties that not only look elegant and attractive but are also suitably resilient, vigorous, and hardy. Whether you're planting in containers

or in the garden, try combining the deep purple blooms of 'Black Pantha' with the creamy white of 'White Heaven' and the striking bi-colour 'Enigma', whose pure white flower with its dark blue base works as the perfect intermediary between the two.

A hardy Agapanthus combination that has worked superbly over the years in our own raised bed is that of the deep blue 'Midnight Star' and the pale, powder-blue 'Hoyland Blue' alongside the bright silver foliage and mauve flowers of 'Silver Moon'. This grouping creates the most striking foliage contrast.

'Black Magic' is the darkest purple in colour of any Agapanthus and combines superbly with campanulatus 'Alba', a pure white Agapanthus that develops a pale pink flush at the tips of the flower. This can be underplanted with the 'Gold strike', which exhibits bright golden variegated foliage and royal-blue flowers held atop highly unusual chocolate-brown stems.

Top: 'Black Pantha'.
Centre: 'Enigma'.
Bottom: 'White Heaven'.

For a simpler yet no less impressive combination, try the late-flowering 'Hole Park Blue' with white 'Peter Franklin'. It is the tried-and-tested simple white and blue colour combination, though with a bit more 'wow' as both varieties are very much giants of the Agapanthus genus and will make a bold statement wherever they are planted. If you desire this soft, demure colour scheme but, perhaps because of limited space, would rather use smaller-growing varieties, try combining blue 'Peter Pan' with white 'Double Diamond' – two small yet effective varieties, which are widely known for their abundant flowering.

For those seeking continuity within a planting scheme and would rather use Agapanthus varieties that fall within the same colour range, the following combinations provide good options.

Dark blue to deep purple – 'Purple Cloud', 'Purple Delight', 'Black Magic', 'Hoyland Chelsea Blue', 'Black Pantha'.

Mid to dark blue – 'Hole Park Blue', 'Midnight Star', 'Lapis Lazuli', 'Brilliant Blue', 'Blue Magic'.

Pale blue to mauve – 'Hoyland Blue', 'Margaret', 'Silver Anniversary', 'Silver Baby'.

Bi-colour – 'Enigma', 'Queen Mum', 'Twister', 'Blueberry Cream'

Top: 'Black Magic'.
Centre: campanulatus 'Alba'.
Bottom: 'Gold Strike'.

Top: 'Peter Pan'.
Centre: 'Double Diamond'.
Bottom: 'Midnight Star' growing amongst ornamental grasses.

White – 'White Heaven', campanulatus 'Alba', 'Peter Franklin', 'Snow Pixie', 'Arctic Star', 'Double Diamond'.

Companion planting

AGAPANTHUS ARE CERTAINLY bold and stunning plants. Yet even here at our nursery we do not grow them in isolation, as their appeal is greatly enhanced when they are grown amongst other types of plants.

Agapanthus is one of the most versatile of perennial plants and they lend themselves to many different styles of garden. Graceful and colourful enough to have a place in a traditional cottage garden or herbaceous border, their bold, architectural form and exotic appearance can be equally effective incorporated into an exotic, tropical-style planting scheme, or else included in contemporary plantings, intermixed with architectural plants and grasses.

Given that Agapanthus are a South African plant, their natural position is surely amongst other members of the *Amaryllidaceae* plant family. An obvious partner is Tulbaghia, the so-called pink Agapanthus, which require practically the same growing conditions as Agapanthus. Tulbaghia are small and demure when compared to Agapanthus, so are often best planted in the forefront of a border or in containers. Doing so ensures that their subtle tones and delicate beauty can be fully appreciated. A superb combination is the deep pink Tulbaghia 'Dark Beauty', the pale mauve 'Elaine Ann', and the highly scented white and yellow 'Scented Beauty'. A real benefit of Tulbaghia is that many varieties are very free flowering and once established will often flower for many months, adding a splash of much-needed colour and interest to even the dullest of days.

Another natural companion of Agapanthus are the truly spectacular autumn-flowering Nerines and Amarines, which are well known for their vivid pink blooms. Try combining these with late-flowering Agapanthus varieties such as 'Hole Park Blue', 'Peter Franklin', and 'Hoyland Blue' as they are usually in flower at the same time during early autumn. The warm colours of Nerines and Amarines contrast wonderfully with the cool blues and whites of Agapanthus, while the close similarity in flower shape and form adds continuity to the planting scheme. Even if traditional summer-flowering Agapanthus are used, it is well worth interplanting them with Nerines and Amarines, both in the border or in containers. When the Agapanthus are fading away and going to seed, the Nerines and Amarines will begin flowering, thus continuing the colour and interest through autumn and early winter.

The sheer amount of other garden plants that make excellent companions for Agapanthus could alone fill this entire volume. There are certainly no fixed rules to dictate which plants you should include in the garden. Even so, we have opted to include lists of what we have found to be excellent companions for Agapanthus and

Above left: Tulbaghia violacea

Above right: Tulbaghia 'Scented Beauty'.

Centre: Tulbaghia 'Purple Eye'.

Bottom: Agapanthus with Nerines and Amarines.

we have grouped them into categories according to the type of garden you wish to achieve. Many of the plants we have listed are indeed interchangeable with other categories, though it is worth keeping in mind that the choice of companion plants often depends upon the style of garden you wish to accomplish.

Top: Autumn flowering Amarine Belladiva.

Centre: Autumn flowering Nerine bowdenii.

Bottom: Nerine 'Elegance'.

The South African Garden

Acanthus mollis
Allium christophii
Aloe arborescens
Amarine belladiva
Amaryllis belladonna
Crocosmia x crocosmiiflora 'Star of the East'
Dierama pulcherrimum
Eucomis autumnalis

Gladiolus nanus
Hedychium coccineum
Hemerocallis fulva
Hesperantha coccinea
Kniphofia uvaria
Nerine bowdenii 'Isabel'
Tulbaghia 'Silver Lace'
Watsonia pillansii

The Cottage Garden

Anenome x Hybrida
Angelica gigas
Aquilegia vulgaris
Buxus sempervirens (Clipped Balls)
Delphinium elatum
Euphorbia griffithii 'Fireglow'
Heliopsis helianthoides
Hydrangea macrophylla

Lavendula angustifolia
Perovskia atriplicifolia
Phlox paniculata
Rosmarinus officinale
Salvia patens 'Cambridge Blue'
Vinca major
Verbena bonariensis

The Grass Garden

Arundo donax 'Golden Chain'
Carex comans 'Bronze'
Carex oshimensis 'Evergold'
Festuca glauca
Imperata cylindrica 'Rubra'
Liriope muscari 'Variegata'
Miscanthus sinensis

Ophiopogon planiscapus 'Nigrescens'
Pennisetum villosum
Stipa gigantea
Stipa tenuissima
Uncinia rubra 'Everflame'

The Exotic / Architectural Garden

Beschorneria yuccoides
Canna indica 'Purpurea'
Cordyline australis
Dahlia 'Karma Chocolate'
Echium candicans
Eucomis autumnalis
Fatsia japonica 'Spiders Web'
Hedychium gardnerianum

Musa basjoo
Persicaria microcephala 'Red Dragon'
Phormium tenax 'Back in Black'
Ricinus communis
Trachyarpus fortunei

Agapanthus as a cut flower

AGAPANTHUS ARE OFTEN used in cut flower arrangements. With their vibrant and graceful blooms, it is not difficult to see why. Cut flower Agapanthus are now a multimillion-pound industry. Cut flowers are obtained from the UK, Europe, Asia, South America, Australasia, and their native home of South Africa. The broad range of places from which cut flowers are obtained ensures they are available for most of the year.

Agapanthus are becoming an increasingly desirable choice with commercial flower suppliers and florists alike. This is largely due to the now widespread popularity of Agapanthus as a garden plant. The sheer beauty of Agapanthus makes them a favourite for weddings and other joyful celebrations.

In the home, also, Agapanthus have become very popular in a vase arrangement. Over the years we have made floral arrangements using anything from a single flower up to huge bowls containing hundreds of flower heads. You can purchase Agapanthus cut flowers from most florists, though their range is often limited to one or two varieties at best. If you have some blooms to spare in the garden, we would highly recommend harvesting a few flower heads to arrange within the home. They will prove to be very long lasting and, placed in a conspicuous location, will receive plenty of attention. You can exhibit them in splendid isolation, or mix them in with a broad range of other flowers in a combined floral arrangement.

If you do not have the heart to remove beautiful flower heads from the garden you can still make use of the seed heads, which are a decorative feature in themselves. Many people appreciate the architectural form and attractive russet-brown colour of the seed heads. You may prefer to spray them silver or gold and use them in a festive floral arrangement at Christmas. If you have an eye for the attractive and unusual, the possibilities are truly endless.

A cut flower exhibit at Sandringham Flower Show 2017.

Agapanthus 'Lavender Haze'
Illustration by Leah Bilson

RECOMMENDED VARIETIES

Agapanthus 'Arctic Star'

A traditional yet beautiful variety, Agapanthus 'Arctic Star' was bred at Raveningham Hall in Norfolk by Lady Priscilla Bacon, a passionate plantswoman and breeder of other well-known Agapanthus varieties, 'Midnight Star' being one of them. It is certainly one of the very best pure white examples and demonstrates the breeder's ability to produce varieties that exhibit both beauty and reliability. Agapanthus 'Arctic Star' is a medium-sized deciduous Agapanthus with large, brilliant white flower heads up to 70cm in height. Vigorous, with tall foliage and a spreading habit, 'Arctic Star' will flower in mid to late summer, usually July/August. Agapanthus 'Arctic Star' has unusually large flower heads similar in appearance to many of the giant evergreen types, but is much hardier and can tolerate temperatures as low as -10°C so is well suited to both the garden and containers. Agapanthus 'Arctic Star' looks stunning when planted next to Agapanthus with dark blue or purple flowers.

Agapanthus 'Black Magic'

AGAPANTHUS 'BLACK MAGIC' is certainly not for the faint-hearted and must be one of the most distinctive of all Agapanthus varieties. 'Black Magic' is the darkest variety currently available; the flowers are such

a dark purple colour they seem almost black. It is a large, deciduous Agapanthus with vibrant deep, dark blooms that reach 80cm in height. 'Black Magic' is not only distinctive in colour but also has an unusual pendulous flower head: unlike more upright forms, each individual flower nods gracefully as it opens. 'Black Magic' will flower in mid to late summer, usually July/ August. Agapanthus 'Black Magic' can be grown well in containers. However, if grown in the garden, a deep mulch is advisable to protect from heavy frosts. The deep purple to black blooms look even more impressive when grown next to pale or pure white Agapanthus varieties.

Agapanthus 'Blue Magic'

VERY QUICK TO establish and with an intensity of colour, Agapanthus 'Blue Magic' is a medium-sized deciduous variety with vivid, rich, deep blue flower heads to 70cm in height. Vigorous, with a compact spreading habit, they flower in mid to late summer, usually July/August. Agapanthus 'Blue Magic' is not only

outstandingly beautiful but also, if grown correctly, will flower freely every year. It is also hardy down to -10°C, so is well suited to both the garden and containers. Agapanthus 'Blue Magic' looks superb when planted next to large Agapanthus with pale or pure white blooms.

Agapanthus 'Blueberry Cream'

ONE OF OUR own introductions, Agapanthus 'Blueberry Cream' arose as a variant of the vigorous and hardy 'Midnight Star'. It shares all the same growth habits, yet is dramatically different in flower colour. 'Blueberry Cream' is a medium-sized, deciduous bi-colour Agapanthus that grows to 60cm in height. The flowers contain a dazzling

combination of white, cream, pale blue, and dark blue, with a distinctive purple base to each individual flower. Vigorous, with a spreading habit, they flower in mid to late summer, usually July/August. Agapanthus 'Blueberry Cream' is not only outstandingly attractive but also, if grown correctly, will flower profusely and reliably

each year. It is also hardy down to -15°C; therefore, it is by far the hardiest bi-colour Agapanthus currently available and is well suited to both the garden and containers. Agapanthus 'Blueberry Cream' looks magnificent when planted next to any Agapanthus, be they white, pale blue, dark blue, or purple.

Agapanthus 'Brilliant Blue'

AGAPANTHUS 'BRILLIANT BLUE' is a delightful deciduous variety with, as the name suggests, brilliant, vivid, deep blue flowers, which are small, neat, and compact, to 50cm in height. They flower in late summer, usually July/August. Agapanthus 'Brilliant Blue' is not only attractive, with its compact spreading habit, but is extremely free flowering and produces masses of small flower heads. It is hardy

down to -10°C, so is well suited to both the garden and containers. Agapanthus 'Brilliant Blue', with its deep blue flowers, looks spectacular when planted next to Agapanthus with pale or pure white blooms.

Agapanthus campanulatus 'Alba'

AGAPANTHUS CAMPANULATUS 'ALBA' is a medium-sized deciduous variety, growing to 80cm in height. It has compact, attractive white flower heads with a distinctive pink flush to the petals that becomes even more pronounced as the flowers mature. Vigorous,

with mid-green foliage and a spreading habit, 'Alba' will flower in mid to late summer, usually July/August. 'Alba' not only flowers very reliably but also can tolerate temperatures as low as -10°C, so is well suited to both the garden and containers. Agapanthus 'Alba', with its white and pink-tinged flowers, looks stunning when planted next to any Agapanthus with dark blue or purple flowers.

Agapanthus 'Castle of Mey'

AGAPANTHUS 'CASTLE OF Mey' is an excellent medium-sized deciduous variety that originates from the Windsor Estate. Growing to 70cm in height, it produces masses of small, lavender-blue flowers with a dark blue midrib. 'Castle of Mey' will flower in late summer, usually July/August. Not only does it have an attractive spreading habit, but, if grown correctly, 'Castle of Mey' is extremely free flowering and produces masses of flower heads each year. It is also hardy down to -10°C, so is well suited to both the garden and containers. Agapanthus 'Castle of Mey', with its lavender-blue flowers, looks magnificent when planted next to white, dark blue, or purple Agapanthus.

Agapanthus 'Charlotte'

AGAPANTHUS 'CHARLOTTE' HAS been widely planted and appreciated for many years. It is a small, mid-blue, evergreen variety that produces masses of flowers, which are star shaped with very open petals. The flowers are mid blue with a deep blue central midrib and reach only 50cm in height. 'Charlotte' will flower in summer, usually July/August. They are hardy only down to -5°C; therefore, it is advisable to move them to a sheltered position or wrap in fleece in colder areas of Britain. 'Charlotte' is enormously popular because it is very

free flowering and produces masses of flowers each year. This makes it perfectly suited to medium and large containers, troughs, or the front of borders in mild areas. 'Charlotte' looks wonderful when planted with small white Agapanthus.

Agapanthus 'Double Diamond'

AGAPANTHUS 'DOUBLE DIAMOND' is an exceptional truly dwarf white variety, so has featured on almost all our floral exhibits for many years. 'Double Diamond' reaches only 20cm in height, yet produces masses of short, bright white flowers that have double petals and conspicuous butter-yellow stamens. 'Double Diamond' will flower

in late summer, usually July/August. They are hardy only down to -5°C; therefore, it is advisable to move containers to a sheltered position or wrap in fleece in colder areas of Britain. 'Double Diamond' is extremely petite, yet very free flowering, which makes it perfectly suited to small containers, troughs, the front of borders, or even a rock garden. 'Double Diamond' looks stunning when planted with dwarf blue Agapanthus.

Agapanthus 'Flower of Love'

AGAPANTHUS 'FLOWER OF Love' is a
medium-sized deciduous variety with
vibrant, deep royal-blue blooms, and
reaches 60cm in height. The plant has
a low-spreading habit, and produces
masses of flowers in mid to late
summer, usually July/August. It is also
hardy down to -10 °C, so is well suited
to both the garden and containers.
Agapanthus 'Flower of Love', with its
deep royal-blue flowers, looks splendid
when planted next to Agapanthus with
white or bi-colour blooms.

Agapanthus 'Golden Drop'

AGAPANTHUS 'GOLDEN DROP' is a very distinctive dwarf variegated
variety and exhibits the perfect combination of both attractive
flowers and interesting foliage. 'Golden Drop' is a small, evergreen

Agapanthus with attractive
pale, sky-blue flower heads
up to 30cm in height.
They will flower in mid
to late summer, usually
July/August. Agapanthus
'Golden Drop' not only has
beautiful flowers but also has
stunningly attractive golden-
edged variegated foliage. It

is hardy to -5°C, so it is advisable to move containers to a sheltered
position or wrap in fleece in colder areas of Britain. The small size of

'Golden Drop' makes it perfectly suited to small containers, troughs, the front of borders, or even a rock garden. With characteristic variegated foliage, this variety certainly brightens up any planting scheme and can soften any areas of dense green foliage.

Agapanthus 'Gold Strike'

AGAPANTHUS 'GOLD STRIKE' is a very unusual variegated variety that exhibits the perfect combination of attractive, unique flowers and stunning foliage. 'Gold Strike' is a medium-sized, evergreen

Agapanthus, growing to 60cm, with attractive pale and dark blue striped flowers held upon highly unusual chocolate-brown stems above bright, golden variegated foliage. They will flower in mid to late summer, usually July/ August. Agapanthus 'Gold Strike' is hardy down to -5°C, so it is advisable to move containers to a sheltered position or wrap them in fleece in colder areas of Britain. With characteristic variegated foliage and distinctive chocolate-coloured flower stems, they will certainly brighten up any planting scheme and soften areas of dense green foliage.

Agapanthus 'Graskop'

AGAPANTHUS 'GRASKOP' is one of the most striking of all Agapanthus varieties. It is an extremely tall deciduous Agapanthus. 'Graskop' has vibrant, deep, dark purple to black blooms, and reaches 100cm in height. 'Graskop' has exceptional colour, but also has an unusually compact, small, heavily pendulous flower head, in which, unlike upright forms, each individual flower droops downward as it opens. 'Graskop' has a spreading habit, and will flower in mid to late summer, usually July/August. It is certainly a one-of-a-kind variety and can be grown extremely well in containers. However, if it is to be grown in the garden, a deep mulch

is advisable to protect from heavy frosts. The deep violet-purple blooms look wonderful when grown next to pale or pure white Agapanthus varieties.

Agapanthus 'Hole Park Blue'

NAMED AFTER THE famous Hole Park Gardens in Kent, where it has thrived for over a hundred years, it is always the last Agapanthus variety to flower, in early autumn. Agapanthus 'Hole Park Blue' is a very large evergreen variety with superb alternating mid then deep blue striped flowers. Growing to 120cm in height, with thick

stems and broad, strap-like leaves, Agapanthus 'Hole Park Blue' will flower in late summer to early autumn, usually in September/October. As they are hardy only down to -5°C, it is advisable to move them to a sheltered position or wrap in fleece in colder parts of Britain. Agapanthus 'Hole Park Blue' has one of the largest flower heads of any Agapanthus. It makes

the ideal specimen for medium to large containers, or an impressive border perennial in milder areas. With its large size and royal-blue colour, it looks incredible when planted close to large white Agapanthus.

Agapanthus 'Hoyland Blue'

AGAPANTHUS 'HOYLAND BLUE' is one of our own introductions. We launched it at the RHS Chelsea Flower 2012 and it was featured on the BBC show coverage by Carol Klein and Christine Walkden.

It also received an award of merit at the Courson Flower Show near Paris, France, that same year, and has been one of our most popular varieties ever since. 'Hoyland Blue' is a medium evergreen Agapanthus with pale, powder-blue flowers, dissected by a dark blue stripe. Up to 70cm in height, with compact spreading habit, Agapanthus 'Hoyland Blue' will flower in late summer to early autumn, usually in August/September. We bred Agapanthus 'Hoyland Blue' to be an excellent performer that flowers profusely even when juvenile. It is hardy down to -10°C so is well suited to both the garden and containers. 'Hoyland Blue' looks superb beside Agapanthus with dark blooms. Though attractive at any time of day, it is at its very best at dusk, when the light, bright flowers of 'Hoyland Blue' appear almost luminescent and seem to glow in the twilight.

Agapanthus 'Hoyland Chelsea Blue'

WE LAUNCHED THIS variety in 2013 to celebrate the centenary of the RHS Chelsea Flower Show. It is one of our very own introductions, selected from over ten thousand seed hybrids for both its beauty and reliability. Agapanthus 'Hoyland Chelsea Blue' is a truly breathtaking

large evergreen variety with superb rich, deep blue flowers on stems 80–100cm in height and broad, ridged, strap-like leaves. Agapanthus 'Hoyland Chelsea Blue' will flower in late summer, usually in July/August. As they are hardy only down to -5°C, it is advisable to move them to a sheltered position or wrap in fleece in colder parts of Britain. Agapanthus 'Hoyland Chelsea Blue' has one of the largest flower heads of any Agapanthus. It makes the ideal specimen for medium to large containers, or as an impressive border perennial in milder areas. With its large size and vivid colour, it is even more spectacular when planted next to pure white Agapanthus.

Agapanthus 'Intermedius'

AGAPANTHUS 'INTERMEDIUS' IS a highly unusual variety. It is deciduous and grows to 60cm in height, with vibrant, deep, dark blue to purple blooms. Yet surely the most striking feature of 'Intermedius' must be the flower stems and buds,

which are jet black in colour. 'Intermedius' will flower in mid to late summer, usually July/August. It is also hardy down to -10°C, so is well suited to both the garden and containers. The midnight-black stems and buds are followed by deep blue to purple blooms, which look wonderful when grown next to either white Agapanthus or variegated varieties, as any bright, vibrant foliage contrasts perfectly with the deep colours of 'Intermedius'.

Agapanthus 'Lapis Lazuli'

AGAPANTHUS 'LAPIS LAZULI' is a compact and free-flowering semi-evergreen variety with bright mid-blue flowers that are small and compact, yet plentiful, growing to 60cm in height. Flowering in early

summer, usually June/July, Agapanthus 'Lapis Lazuli' is not only attractive, with a compact, spreading habit, but, if grown correctly, is extremely free flowering and produces masses of small flower heads each year. It is also hardy down to -10°C, so is well suited to both the garden and containers. Agapanthus 'Lapis Lazuli', with its sky-blue flowers, looks magnificent when planted next to any Agapanthus.

Agapanthus 'Little Seb'

ONE OF OUR own recent introductions, Agapanthus 'Little Seb' is an excellent dwarf blue variety. It produces masses of compact, rich dark blue flower heads to only 30cm in height. They flower in midsummer, usually June/July. Agapanthus 'Little Seb' is not only attractive, with a very low- yet rapidly spreading habit, but, if grown correctly, is also extremely free flowering and produces masses of small flower heads. It is deciduous and hardy down to -10°C, so is well suited to rock gardens, the front of borders or small to medium troughs or containers. Agapanthus 'Little Seb', with its rich blue flowers, looks splendid when planted next to dwarf white Agapanthus.

Agapanthus 'Margaret'

ANOTHER OF OUR own introductions, Agapanthus 'Margaret' is a medium-sized deciduous variety with attractive sky-blue flowers with a compact flower head, and reaches 90cm in height. Agapanthus 'Margaret' is vigorous with a spreading habit, and will flower in mid to late summer, usually July to August. Agapanthus 'Margaret' is not only beautiful but is also an excellent performer and will flower profusely and reliably year after year. It is also hardy down to -10°C, so is well suited to both the garden and containers. Agapanthus 'Margaret' is a rich mid-blue colour, so is very versatile

and can be planted with any other Agapanthus variety, whether they are white, pale, or dark in colour, with equal success. We have also produced two new varieties that are variants of 'Margaret': Agapanthus 'Malcolm' has much paler blue flowers than 'Margaret', whilst Agapanthus 'Pink Pantha' has very distinct lilac/lavender flowers. Both of these interesting new varieties grow in exactly the same way as 'Margaret' but have distinctly different flower colours.

Agapanthus 'Midnight Dream'

AGAPANTHUS 'MIDNIGHT DREAM' is one of the most eye-catching and distinctive of all Agapanthus varieties. It certainly stole the show on our Chelsea Flower Show 2013 exhibit. Reaching 70cm in height, it is a medium-sized deciduous Agapanthus and, as the name 'Midnight Dream' implies, has vibrant, deep, dark violet-purple blooms.

'Midnight Dream' is not only distinctive in colour but also has an unusual semi-pendulous flower head in which, unlike more upright forms, each individual flower nods gracefully as it opens. 'Midnight Dream' has a low-spreading habit, and will flower in mid to late summer, usually July/August. Agapanthus 'Midnight Dream' is gorgeous and distinctive. It can be grown well in containers. If grown in the garden, however, a deep mulch is advisable to protect from heavy frosts. The deep violet-purple blooms look wonderful when grown next to pale or pure white Agapanthus varieties.

Agapanthus 'Midnight Star'

AN OLD YET stunning variety, Agapanthus 'Midnight Star' was bred at Raveningham Hall in Norfolk by Lady Priscilla Bacon, a passionate plantswoman and breeder. It is certainly one of our favourite varieties and exhibits the perfect combination of beauty and reliability. 'Midnight Star' is a medium-sized, deciduous Agapanthus with vivid, rich, navy-blue flower heads to 60cm in height. Vigorous with a compact spreading habit, they flower in mid to late summer, usually July/August. Not only is Agapanthus 'Midnight Star'

strikingly attractive but also, if grown correctly, it will flower profusely and reliably every year. It is hardy down to -15°C so is well suited to both the garden and containers. Agapanthus 'Midnight Star' looks magnificent when planted next to Agapanthus with pale blue or pure white blooms.

Agapanthus 'Moonlight Star'

AGAPANTHUS 'MOONLIGHT STAR' is a medium-size evergreen variety, with very rounded flower heads and unique, star-like, mid-blue flowers that have a dark blue stripe. Growing to 70cm in height, they have thick, erect stems

and broad, strap-like leaves. Agapanthus 'Moonlight Star' will flower in mid to late summer, usually July/August. This variety is hardy only down to -5°C, so it is advisable to move containers to a sheltered position or wrap in fleece in colder parts of Britain. Agapanthus 'Moonlight Star' has large and impressive flower heads, which makes it the ideal specimen for medium to large containers, or an impressive border perennial in milder areas. With a multitude of flowers of the most striking blue colour, it looks incredible when planted close to large white Agapanthus.

Agapanthus 'Peter Franklin'

AGAPANTHUS 'PETER FRANKLIN' is a very large evergreen variety with flowers up to 120cm in height, with thick stems and large, broad, strap-like leaves. The blooms are extremely large and are

a striking brilliant pure white. Agapanthus 'Peter Franklin' will flower in late summer, usually in August/ September. They are hardy only down to -5°C; therefore, it is advisable to move them to a sheltered position or wrap in fleece in colder areas of Britain. Agapanthus 'Peter Franklin', with its impressive size and arresting colour, makes the ideal specimen for medium to large containers, or a striking border perennial in milder parts of Britain. The stunning white flower complements most other Agapanthus varieties, though it is particularly effective when planted close to deep blue or purple Agapanthus.

Agapanthus 'Peter Pan'

AGAPANTHUS 'PETER PAN' is a traditional, yet still widely planted, dwarf blue variety. It is a small evergreen Agapanthus that produces masses of small, sky-blue flowers reaching only 40cm in height.

'Peter Pan' will flower in late summer, usually July/August. This variety is hardy only down to -5°C; therefore, it is advisable to move containers to a sheltered position or wrap in fleece in colder areas of Britain. 'Peter Pan' is extremely small yet boasts plenty of flowers, which makes it perfectly suited to small containers, troughs, the front of borders, and even rock gardens. 'Peter Pan' looks wonderful when planted with dwarf white Agapanthus.

Agapanthus praecox

AGAPANTHUS PRAECOX IS the wild species that a great many varieties

originate from. It is a very large evergreen Agapanthus with attractive flowers varying in colour from pale to navy blue, to 120cm in height, with thick stems and broad, strap-like leaves. Agapanthus praecox will flower in summer, in July/August. As they are hardy only down to -5°C, it is advisable to move them to a sheltered position or wrap in fleece in colder parts of Britain. The plant has very large showy blooms. It makes the ideal specimen for medium to large containers, or an impressive border perennial in milder areas. With its large size and blue colour, it looks incredible when planted close to any large white Agapanthus.

Agapanthus 'Purple Cloud'

AGAPANTHUS 'PURPLE CLOUD' is a very distinctive variety and combines remarkable size with striking flower colour. 'Purple

Cloud' has strong, vibrant, deep purple blooms, growing to 120cm in height, and masses of narrow, mid-green leaves. It is not only outstanding in colour but also has an unusual semi-pendulous flower head, in which, unlike more upright forms, each individual flower nods gracefully as it opens. 'Purple Cloud' will flower in mid to late summer, usually July/August. This variety is hardy down to -5°C, so it is advisable to move containers to a sheltered position or wrap in fleece in colder parts of Britain. Agapanthus 'Purple Cloud' is remarkably tall for a plant with such an unusual form and dark purple flowers. It makes the ideal specimen for medium to large containers or an impressive border perennial in milder areas. With its large size and intense purple colour, it looks stunningly attractive when planted close to pale blue or pure white Agapanthus.

Agapanthus 'Purple Delight'

AGAPANTHUS 'PURPLE DELIGHT' is an eye-catching variety that combines wonderful form with outstanding flower colour. 'Purple

Delight' has strong, vibrant, deep
purple blooms to 90cm in height and
masses of mid-green leaves. 'Purple
Delight' is not only outstanding
in colour but also has large, neat,
rounded flower heads. 'Purple
Delight' will flower in mid to late
summer, usually July/August. As
it is hardy only down to -5°C, it
is advisable to move containers to

a sheltered position or wrap in fleece in colder parts of Britain.
Agapanthus 'Purple Delight' makes the ideal specimen for medium to
large containers, or an impressive border perennial in milder areas.
With its large size and intense purple colour, it looks magnificent
when planted close to pale, blue or pure white Agapanthus.

Agapanthus 'Queen Mum'

AGAPANTHUS 'QUEEN MUM' is a very large evergreen variety with
flowers up to 120cm in height, thick stems, and large, broad, strap-
like leaves. The blooms are stunningly bi-coloured with large, pure

white flowers that have a
distinctive purple/blue base
to each individual flower.
Agapanthus 'Queen Mum' will
flower in late summer, usually
in July/August. They are hardy
down to -5°C. Therefore, it is
advisable to move them to a
sheltered position or wrap in

fleece in colder areas of Britain. Agapanthus 'Queen Mum' is certainly
one of the largest and most impressive Agapanthus varieties, making

it the ideal specimen for medium to large containers, or as a striking border perennial in milder areas. The two-tone flower complements most other Agapanthus varieties, whether they are blue or white.

Agapanthus 'Sandringham'

AGAPANTHUS 'SANDRINGHAM' IS a lovely deciduous variety that has brilliant violet-blue flowers with a deep blue midrib. The flower heads are neat and compact, growing to 60cm in height and

flowering in midsummer, usually July/August. If grown correctly, Agapanthus 'Sandringham' is extremely free flowering and produces small yet plentiful flower heads. It is also hardy down to -10°C, so is well suited to both the garden and containers. Agapanthus 'Sandringham', with its two-tone deep blue flowers, looks magnificent when planted next to Agapanthus with pale or pure white blooms.

Agapanthus 'Silver Anniversary'

AGAPANTHUS 'SILVER ANNIVERSARY' was launched in 2010 to celebrate Steve and Elaine's own 25th wedding anniversary. Eye-catching and distinctive, 'Silver Anniversary' boasts plenty of attractive pale silver-grey flowers. It is a mid-sized, deciduous Agapanthus, to 70cm in height. Not only is 'Silver Anniversary' a superb colour, but it is vigorous and produces plentiful blooms, flowering in mid to late summer, usually July/August. It is also hardy down to -10°C, so is well suited to both the garden and containers. The subtle blooms look exceptional when planted alongside Agapanthus varieties that have dark blue or purple blooms.

Agapanthus 'Silver Baby'

AGAPANTHUS 'SILVER BABY' is one of the most popular pale-coloured varieties. 'Silver Baby' is a small evergreen Agapanthus with pale, silver to white flowers, with distinctive blue edges. It grows to 50cm in height, with a compact, low-spreading habit. Agapanthus 'Silver Baby' will flower in late summer, usually July/August. This variety is an excellent performer, which flowers profusely even when juvenile. Its compact habit  makes it well suited to containers. It is hardy down to -5°C, so should be protected in very cold regions. 'Silver Baby' looks superb beside Agapanthus with dark blooms.

Agapanthus 'Silver Moon'

INTRODUCED SOME YEARS ago by Notcutts Garden Centre, Agapanthus 'Silver Moon' is certainly one of the very best variegated varieties and exhibits the perfect combination of beauty and reliability as it is the hardiest variegated Agapanthus available. 'Silver Moon' is a medium-sized, deciduous Agapanthus with attractive rich lavender-blue flower heads, up to 70cm in height. Vigorous, with a compact spreading habit, they will flower in mid to late summer, usually July/August. Agapanthus 'Silver Moon' not only has beautiful flowers but, also, has stunningly attractive silver-edged variegated foliage; it certainly brightens up any planting scheme and softens any areas of dense green foliage. Hardy down to -15°C, it is well suited to both the garden and containers. Agapanthus 'Silver Moon', with its splendid flowers and distinctive foliage, looks magnificent when planted amongst any Agapanthus.

Agapanthus 'Snow Pixie'

AGAPANTHUS 'SNOW PIXIE' is an evergreen dwarf white variety that reaches only 40cm in height but more than compensates for its small stature by producing masses of short, bright white flowers. 'Snow

Pixie' will flower in mid to late summer, usually July/August. They are hardy only down to -5°C; therefore, it is advisable to move containers to a sheltered position or wrap in fleece in colder parts of Britain. 'Snow Pixie' is very compact, yet free flowering, which makes it perfectly suited to small containers, troughs, the front of borders, or even a rock garden. 'Snow Pixie' looks wonderful when planted with dwarf blue Agapanthus.

Agapanthus 'Strawberry Ice'

AGAPANTHUS 'STRAWBERRY ICE' is an interesting medium-sized, evergreen variety with very full flower heads to 60cm in height, held

upon strong, thick stems. The
flowers are a bright, brilliant
white colour with a distinctive
pink flush to the petals, which
becomes even more pronounced as
the flowers mature. Agapanthus
'Strawberry Ice' will flower in
late summer, usually July/August.
They are hardy only down to -5°C;
therefore, it is advisable to move
them to a sheltered position or
wrap in fleece in colder areas of

Britain. Agapanthus 'Strawberry Ice' makes the ideal specimen for
medium-size containers, or an effective border perennial in milder
areas. The unique white to pink blooms complement most other
Agapanthus varieties, whether they are dark blue, pale, or bi-colour.

Agapanthus 'Taw Valley'

AGAPANTHUS 'TAW VALLEY' is a
charming deciduous variety with
rich, vivid, royal-blue open flower
heads to 80cm in height. They flower
in late summer, usually July/August.
Not only is the strong spreading
habit of the plant attractive, but,
if grown correctly, this variety
is extremely free flowering and

produces masses of handsome flower heads. It is also hardy down to
-10°C, so is well suited to both the garden and containers. Agapanthus
'Taw Valley', with its deep royal-blue flowers, looks splendid when
planted next to Agapanthus with pale or pure white blooms.

Agapanthus 'Twister'

ONE OF THE very best bi-colour varieties on the market, Agapanthus 'Twister' is semi-evergreen and much smaller in size than both

'Queen Mum' and 'Enigma', though no less impressive. The blooms are stunningly bi-coloured with masses of compact flower heads to 60cm. The pure white flowers have a distinct purple/blue base to each individual flower. Agapanthus 'Twister' will flower in late summer, usually July/August. 'Twister' is one of the hardiest bi-colour varieties available and can tolerate temperatures as low as -10°C, so is well suited to both the garden and containers. The two-tone flower complements most other Agapanthus varieties, whether they are purple, blue, or white.

Agapanthus 'White Heaven'

AGAPANTHUS 'WHITE HEAVEN' is a very large evergreen variety with flowers up to 100cm in height, with thick stems and large, broad, strap-like leaves. The blooms are extremely large and an exquisite creamy white colour. Agapanthus 'White Heaven' will flower in late summer, usually July/August. They are hardy only down to -5°C; therefore, it is advisable to move them to a sheltered position or wrap in fleece in colder areas of Britain. Agapanthus 'White Heaven' is certainly the largest and most impressive white Agapanthus, making it the ideal specimen for medium to large containers, or as a striking border perennial in milder areas. The stunning white flower complements most other Agapanthus varieties, whether they are dark blue, pale or bi-colour.

Agapanthus 'Windsor Grey'

AGAPANTHUS 'WINDSOR GREY' is a very distinctive variety that combines unusual form with an interesting flower colour. 'Windsor Grey' is a tall, deciduous Agapanthus that has subtle, pale, blue-grey flowers, faintly tinged with violet, to 90 cm in height and masses of upright, green leaves. 'Windsor Grey' is not only outstanding in colour but also has an unusual semi-pendulous flower head, in which, unlike more upright forms, each individual flower nods gracefully as it opens. 'Windsor Grey' will flower in mid to late summer, usually July/August. It is also hardy down to  -10°C, so is well suited to both the garden and containers. Agapanthus 'Windsor Grey' is tall for a plant with such an unusual colour and form so makes the ideal specimen for medium to large containers, or an impressive border perennial. With its large size and distinct form, it looks stunningly attractive when planted close to Agapanthus with dark blue or purple blooms.

Agapanthus 'Yorkshire Rose'

AGAPANTHUS 'YORKSHIRE ROSE' is a medium-sized deciduous variety, growing to 50cm in height, with masses of beautiful compact white flower heads. Vigorous, with mid-green foliage and a low-spreading

habit, 'Yorkshire Rose' will flower in mid to late summer, usually July/August. 'Yorkshire Rose' is not only attractive and free flowering but is also very hardy and can tolerate temperatures as low as -10°C, so is well suited to both the garden and containers. Agapanthus 'Yorkshire Rose', with its brilliant white colour, looks particularly magnificent when planted next to Agapanthus varieties with dark blue or purple flowers.

Tulbaghia 'Scented Beauty'
Illustration by Leah Bilson

TROUBLESHOOTING

Over the years, we have acquired a considerable amount of knowledge and experience in Agapanthus growing. In that time our expertise has been sought by a broad range of people, from experienced professional gardeners and plant scientists to enthusiastic novice gardeners who have just purchased their very first Agapanthus. To reflect this, below is a list of the most relevant and frequently asked questions we have received in our years as Agapanthus specialists.

We have endeavoured to include short yet concise answers to all these questions. Far more comprehensive answers are given in the main body of this volume; however, we feel this section will be of use, whether to provide a quick-fix answer to a specific question or to simply jog the memory if some time has passed since this book was last read.

Frequently asked questions

My Agapanthus have green leaves, but no flowers – why?
The most common reason for Agapanthus not flowering is lack of, or incorrect, feeding, though other common causes are prolonged drought, dense shade, or an overly pot-bound plant. A juvenile plant that is struggling to fill a large pot may also take much longer to reach flowering size.

Should my Agapanthus lose its leaves during winter?
It depends on the type; some species are naturally evergreen and keep their foliage all year round, while others are deciduous and die back to ground level each autumn.

How often should I pot on my Agapanthus?
You should pot on your Agapanthus approximately every two years to keep them vigorous and healthy.

I have been told Agapanthus need to be pot bound to flower – is this true?
This is true for young Agapanthus as they can be kept in the same pot for around two years with no adverse effects, though not indefinitely as some people believe. Overly pot-bound plants often exhibit a marked reduction in both vigour and the number of flowers each year.

How often should I divide my Agapanthus?
You should divide your Agapanthus approximately every four to six years. It is especially important for container-grown Agapanthus as they will eventually fill even the largest of containers, so dividing not only encourages vigorous growth and flowering but also keeps container-grown plants more manageable.

What time of year should I divide my Agapanthus?
Division is best done in spring.

I'm moving to a new house in October; can I dig up and divide my Agapanthus to take with me despite the season?
Yes, Agapanthus can be successfully divided in autumn. But ensure good drainage is provided.

Why did I lose my Agapanthus in the garden during winter?
The most common reason is not frost damage, as most people believe, but inadequate drainage. Agapanthus require good drainage and may rot if they are 'stood' in water during winter, which is often the case with heavy clay soils.

How frost hardy are Agapanthus?
Evergreen types are usually hardy to around -5°C and deciduous types to -10 to -15°C, though mulching and fleecing can add further protection.

Will my Agapanthus grow in shade?
All Agapanthus can grow well in light, dappled shade, though flowering can be much reduced in dense shade.

Is my garden too acidic or alkaline for Agapanthus?
As long as drainage and nutrition are adequate, Agapanthus are not pH sensitive and will grow in most soils.

My Agapanthus has finished flowering; do I need to cut the seed heads off?
If you think the seed heads look attractive, or you want to harvest the seeds, you can leave the seed heads on until late in the year. If not, you can remove the seed heads immediately after flowering with no adverse effects whatsoever. Always ensure high potash feeds are

applied, to encourage flowering.

How long does it take an Agapanthus to flower from seed?
It usually takes three to four years to flower an Agapanthus from seed.

Can Agapanthus change colour?
No, Agapanthus do not change colour. However, if you allow them to set seed, the offspring may germinate and grow within the parent 'clump' and may ultimately be a different colour from the parent plant.

I now have far fewer flowers on my Agapanthus than last year – what's wrong?
It is likely over pot bound. Divide the following spring, repot or replant, and feed with a high potash feed regularly to encourage flowering.

What is the correct potting mix for Agapanthus in containers?
The ideal mix for Agapanthus is a 2:1 ratio of two parts multipurpose compost or John Innes No. 2 or 3 to one part horticultural grit.

Can I overwinter my Agapanthus in the house to protect it?
No, a house is far too warm for an Agapanthus, which requires a cool winter to flower well.

Where is the best place to overwinter my Agapanthus?
An unheated glasshouse, coldframe, or in the lee of a sheltered wall is ideal.

Can I overwinter my Agapanthus in a garage or shed without windows?
Deciduous varieties, which die back to ground level and go completely dormant, can be kept fairly dry and in the darkness during winter. Evergreen varieties do require some light during winter.

If I keep them under cover, do I need to water my Agapanthus during winter?

Deciduous types require little or no water during winter. Evergreen types need a little more water, so should be kept slightly moist to maintain their foliage.

Do Agapanthus make good cut flowers?

Agapanthus make attractive and long-lasting cut flowers.

Do Agapanthus grow from a bulb?

Often confused with the vaguely similar-looking yet unrelated Alliums, Agapanthus actually grow from a fleshy, elongated root structure known as a rhizome.

Why is my Agapanthus flowering pink?

It is certainly not an Agapanthus – it is likely either a Tulbaghia or a Nerine, both of which are related to Agapanthus and have the common name 'pink Agapanthus'. Agapanthus do come in shades of mauve, and some white Agapanthus have pink tips, but there is currently no such thing as a truly pink Agapanthus.

Can I plant different Agapanthus varieties in the same pot?

Yes, often the forms and colours contrast and complement each other well. Late-flowering varieties can also serve to extend the flowering season.

Are Agapanthus prone to pest and disease problems?

They are generally trouble-free, but some pests and diseases can cause very occasional, minor damage to Agapanthus (see section on pests and diseases).

Slugs and snails have devoured my Hostas; will they be after my Agapanthus next?

No, though slugs and snails often take shelter in the cool, moist areas beneath the foliage. They seldom, if ever, seem to attack Agapanthus.

How long does Agapanthus seed keep for?

It is always best to sow Agapanthus seed fresh, within the first year of harvest. After the first year, some seeds will still grow, but the germination rate will be much reduced.

Do Agapanthus only flower in summer?

Largely yes, though there are a few late-flowering varieties, such as 'Hoyland Blue', 'Hole Park Blue', and 'Peter Franklin', that bloom well into autumn.

Will the wind flatten my Agapanthus?

No – despite their somewhat fragile, top-heavy appearance, most Agapanthus stems are rigid and robust and can withstand strong winds and exposed sites.

Are there only white or blue Agapanthus flowers?

Strictly speaking yes, though there is a considerable range of shades within that spectrum, from pure white with flushes of pink, to steely grey, pale sky blue, mauve, navy blue, indigo, and deep purples that border on black. There are even bi-colour varieties available with shades of blue and white within the same flower.

Can I feed my Agapanthus with a general-purpose plant food, when I feed my other perennials?

It is not a good idea as there is often far too much nitrogen in balanced plant food, resulting in copious amounts of lush green foliage, yet with few or no flowers. For best results the regular application of a high-potash feed is best. We manufacture our own brand of Agapanthus feed, which is very high in potash and contains other nutrients essential for healthy plant growth.

Is there such a thing as a dwarf Agapanthus?

Yes, but you must be sure to select a truly dwarf variety, not just a small plant that will ultimately grow large. Well-known and reliable dwarf Agapanthus varieties such as the blue 'Peter Pan' and the white

'Double Diamond' are popular choices for gardeners.

Are Agapanthus bee and pollinator friendly?
Yes, Agapanthus are very good for bees, pollinators, and wildlife in general.

How can I tell if my Agapanthus is evergreen or deciduous?
Evergreen types are usually characterised by large, broad fleshy leaves that persist all year round, usually held upon thick, fleshy stems. Deciduous types are often characterised by having much narrower, finer leaves than evergreen types. They exhibit a multitude of stems, but of a much smaller size than a typical evergreen Agapanthus, and die back to ground level in autumn.

I was told tomato feeds are best for Agapanthus – is this true?
No, it is much better to use a specialist Agapanthus feed, which has a significantly higher potash content than tomato feed. Whilst tomato feed is usually a better option than using a balanced feed, tomato feeds do not have sufficient potash levels to fully satisfy Agapanthus, which are incredibly hungry for potash.

Why does my variegated Agapanthus never flower?
It is probably an old-fashioned Agapanthus variety called 'Tinkerbell', which has attractive silver variegated leaves yet seldom, if ever, flowers. Modern variegated varieties such as 'Silver Moon', 'Gold Strike', and 'Golden Drop' both have attractive variegated foliage and flower readily.

Are variegated Agapanthus frost tender?
No, evergreen variegated varieties such as 'Gold Strike' and 'Golden Drop' are hardy to around -5°C. The deciduous 'Silver Moon' is very tough and is hardy to around -15°C.

I brought an Agapanthus 'root' back from Madeira – is it frost hardy?

It is likely a form of praecox, which are said to be hardy to about -5°C. As a note of caution, however, it must be considered that these Agapanthus will have been grown in a warm, frost-free climate and, as such, will not have been 'hardened off' and so may not fare as well in winter as British-grown Agapanthus praecox.

I love dark flowers; which Agapanthus variety is the darkest of them all?

'Black Magic' is the darkest variety currently available. The flower colour is such a dark purple that they seem almost black.

I have been told that Agapanthus grow like weeds in Australia and New Zealand – will they be invasive in my garden?

No, whilst it is true that certain wild species and hybrids are very rampant in Australia and New Zealand, in the cooler, temperate climate of Britain, Agapanthus are much slower growing and are not at all invasive.

Naturalised Agapanthus in South Africa.

INDEX